Disclaimer

This biography book is a work of nonfiction based on the public life of a famous person. The author has used publicly available information to create this work. While the author has thoroughly researched the subject and attempted to depict it accurately, it is not meant to be an exhaustive study of the subject. The views expressed in this book are those of the author alone and do not necessarily reflect those of any organization associated with the subject. This book should not be taken as an endorsement, legal advice, or any other form of professional advice. This book was written for entertainment purposes only.

Vladimir Putin

By United Library

https://campsite.bio/unitedlibrary

Table of Contents

Introduction

Explore the enigmatic political journey of Vladimir Vladimirovich Putin, the formidable Russian leader whose influence has been felt across the globe. Born on October 7, 1952, Putin's trajectory from a career in the KGB, where he served as a foreign intelligence officer for 16 years, to becoming the President of Russia in 1999, marks a tale of strategic ascent and enduring dominance.

Delve into Putin's pivotal role in reshaping Russia's political landscape, holding continuous positions as president or prime minister since 1999. From his early days in Saint Petersburg to his role in the administration of President Boris Yeltsin, Putin's political prowess became evident. His presidency, marked by economic reforms and a robust growth rate, saw Russia confront internal conflicts, including the conflict with Chechen separatists.

Witness Putin's return to power in 2012 amid allegations of fraud and protests, and his subsequent reelections in 2018 and beyond. His tenure has been defined by both economic achievements and controversies, from overseeing military conflicts with Georgia to the annexation of Crimea and military intervention in Syria.

However, Putin's leadership has sparked international condemnation, particularly for the invasion of Ukraine in February 2022 and the subsequent annexation of Ukrainian territories. The International Criminal Court issued an arrest warrant for Putin in March 2023, alleging war crimes during the conflict.

This book navigates through Putin's intricate political maneuverings, shedding light on the complex geopolitical landscape he has shaped, and the controversies surrounding his rule, including democratic backsliding, human rights violations, and accusations of corruption. As the longest-serving Russian president, Putin's impact on Russia and the world is scrutinized, making this a compelling exploration of a leader whose legacy is both enduring and contentious.

Vladimir Putin

Vladimir Vladimirovich Putin, born on October 7, 1952 in Leningrad (now St. Petersburg), is a Russian statesman. Since 1999, he has been the central figure in the Russian nation's executive branch, alternating as President of the Government (1999-2000 and 2008-2012) and President of the Russian Federation (acting from 1999 to 2000, and full President from 2000 to 2008 and since 2012).

An officer in the KGB, the USSR's main intelligence service, he was stationed in Dresden at the time of the fall of the Berlin Wall. He began his political career as mayor of St. Petersburg, before becoming one of President Boris Yeltsin's closest advisors, who made him director of the Federal Security Service (formerly the KGB) in 1998, then president of the Russian government the following year.

Following Boris Yeltsin's resignation on December 31, 1999, he took over as acting President of the Russian Federation. He became full President on May 7, 2000, after winning the early presidential election. During his first term, he launched a series of major reforms to restore the power of a country in economic crisis, which had lost influence in the world. He led a recovery of the national economy and an institutional policy aimed at concentrating presidential powers. He was widely re-elected in 2004.

In 2008, as the Constitution prohibited him from running for a third consecutive term, he supported the presidential candidacy of his first deputy prime minister, Dmitry Medvedev. Once elected head of state, Medvedev appointed Putin prime minister, who also took over the leadership of the United Russia party and remained the country's strongman, with a president who appeared to be more liberal. Frequently accused of authoritarianism, Putin was significantly challenged for the first time following the 2011 parliamentary elections.

Running in the 2012 presidential election with the support of the outgoing Medvedev, he returned to the presidency for a six-year term. During this period, he intends to restore Russian influence on the international stage. On the one hand, in 2014, in the context of the war in the Donbass and following a disputed local referendum, he allowed the annexation to Russia of the autonomous republic of Crimea, from its Ukrainian neighbor, an act often considered to violate international law. He also sent an expeditionary force to fight in the Syrian civil war, in support of Bashar al-Assad's regime.

He was elected to a fourth term in the 2018 presidential election. Two years later, he had a referendum passed on the non-limitation of presidential terms, which would allow him to remain in power until 2036. In February 2022, he launched a military invasion of Ukraine after recognizing the separatist republics of Donetsk and Lugansk. A few months later, he announced a partial mobilization, annexed four regions in eastern and southern Ukraine, and threatened to use nuclear weapons. In 2023, the International Criminal Court issued an arrest warrant for war crimes and the illegal transfer of Ukrainian children.

Under Vladimir Putin's rule, Russia has experienced an erosion of democracy and a slide towards authoritarianism. The country is characterized by endemic corruption and numerous human rights abuses, including the imprisonment and repression of political opponents, the intimidation and suppression of independent media, and the absence of free elections. In 2023, Vladimir Putin will be the second-longest-serving European president, after Alexander Lukashenko of Belarus.

Personal situation

Childhood and adolescence

Vladimir Putin came from a modest working-class family, of which he was the third and last child. His parents, Vladimir Spiridonovitch Putin (1911-1999) and Maria Ivanovna Putina, née Chelomova (1911-1998), had two sons before him, Albert Putin and Viktor Putin, born in the late 1930s and 1940 respectively, but both died in infancy during the siege of Leningrad. Vladimir Spiridonovitch Putin, a Red Army soldier from 1941, belonged to the divisions positioned around Leningrad, along the Neva River. During the fighting against the German Army, he was seriously wounded in the left leg. According to Vladimir Putin, his mother survived the 872-day siege of Leningrad during the war, although for a time she was left for dead and rescued by her husband on his return from hospital. After the war, the couple worked at the Leningrad railway factory.

His paternal grandparents were peasants from the hamlet of Pominovo, part of the village of Tourguinovo (Tver Oblast), north of Moscow, who had lived there since the village was founded in the XVIIe century. According to Vladimir Putin's biographer, his grandfather, Spiridon Putin, was the first of the line to be born after the abolition of serfdom in the Tsarist Empire. Spiridon, whom Vladimir Putin has said is the family member he most admires, is said to have been a cook to the Romanovs, and later to Lenin and Stalin" .

A few days after his birth, Vladimir Putin's mother secretly requested that her son be baptized in Transfiguration Cathedral, even though baptism could be severely punished in the Soviet Union, an institutionally atheistic state. He is a mediocre student according to some, average according to others, and a brawler" . In his youth, Vladimir Putin practiced sambo (Russian wrestling) and judo from the age of 12. He was Leningrad sambo champion; in 1973, he was awarded the title of master of sambo sports, and in 1976 of judo' . He also enjoys ice hockey.

Putin studied law at the University of Leningrad (now St Petersburg State University), where he studied Thomas Hobbes, John Locke and Immanuel Kant, among others. He graduated in 1975 with a dissertation on "The principle of most-favored-nation trade in international law". Anatoli Sobchak, then a professor at the university, was his academic supervisor.

Putin speaks fluent German, having lived and worked for several years in the German Democratic Republic, but has very little command of English and prefers to use interpreters when conversing with English speakers' .

Career as a KGB officer

According to his own account, Vladimir Putin tried unsuccessfully to join the KGB at the age of 16. After university studies and a brief initial training, of which little is known [réf.] , he joined the KGB's decentralized territorial service - the KGB directorate for the city of Leningrad and its region, where he served for several years, first as a subordinate, then as an operational officer in the local counter-espionage service, responsible in particular for the political police's fight against dissidents and other "anti-Soviet elements" (under the patronage of the KGB's fifth directorate).

Like all other European special services at the time, the KGB only sent married men on foreign postings, a condition designed in principle to keep out homosexuals and avoid liaisons with foreign women. Putin married in 1983.

With the rank of major (Russian: Майор, *maïor*), in 1984 he was sent for a year's training at the KGB's Andropov Institute (or Red Flag Institute, *Krasnoznamenny Inst40oule* - KI) in Moscow, ostensibly to become a spy. During this period, he goes by the code name "Platov" and acts as volunteer leader of his unit of officers-in-training.

On completion of his training at the KI, Putin was not assigned to a unit at KGB headquarters in Moscow, but returned to Leningrad to the local unit under the supervision of the KGB's first directorate general, the foreign intelligence service. He then moved to the KGB's "active reserve" to prepare for an operational mission in the German Democratic Republic (GDR) in the Eastern Bloc.

From August 1985, his first foreign posting was in Dresden in the GDR, officially as a consular employee, but in fact to recruit spies as a *major* (commander) in the Russian secret service. Among other things, he tried to coerce a medical professor into giving him access to a study on deadly poisons that leave almost no trace, by blackmailing him with pornographic material. After the fall of the Berlin Wall, he prevented Germans from entering KGB offices in order to ransack them and loot the files, destroying the documents himself afterwards. He was recalled to Russia in February 1990, in the context of German reunification. According to the German media *Correctiv*, he owes his return to the fact that Werner Grossmann, the last head of the GDR's foreign espionage services, revealed to his KGB colleagues that Putin was recruiting GDR agents whose cover had been blown, creating a major risk for the KGB.

Political ascent

With German reunification and the dismantling of KGB facilities in the German Democratic Republic, Lieutenant-Colonel (in Russian: Подполковник, *podpolkovnik*) Putin returned to Leningrad to resume his operational service in the local KGB leadership with cover as international affairs advisor to the rector of Leningrad University, Anatoli Sobchak (who had been his professor fifteen years earlier at the provincial capital's law faculty).

From the KGB to St Petersburg City Hall (1991-1995)

In June 1991, Sobchak, democratically elected head of the Leningrad soviet (the city's mayor), invited Putin to become his international affairs advisor: Putin accepted while remaining in his KGB post. It is possible that in August 1991, Putin played a role in the delicate negotiations between the Leningrad KGB and the military structures linked to the Kremlin putschists. Putin claims to have officially resigned from the KGB on August 20, 1991, during the coup against Gorbachev, but his resignation was not accepted.

His resignation from the KGB was only later accepted, but there is no official evidence to prove it unambiguously.

From 1992 to 1996, Putin was one of the most influential figures in municipal politics, Sobchak's "éminence grise": he became head of external relations at City Hall and, from 1994, first deputy. According to former investigator Andrei Zykov, "Anatoli Sobchak and his deputy Vladimir Putin became, in a way, the heads of the St. Petersburg mafia", and it was at this time that a "model of corruption" was born around Vladimir Putin, whose entourage then accompanied him all the way to the Kremlin.

In autumn 1995, Sobchak appointed him chairman of the local branch of Our Home Russia - in Russian: Наш дом - Россия, *Nash dom - Rossiya (NDR)* - the party of Government Chairman (Prime Minister) Chernomyrdin. He is in charge of leading the parliamentary election campaign in the region on behalf of NDR. He remained loyal to Sobchak despite the latter's defeat in the 1996 municipal elections, refusing to work with Vladimir Yakovlev. He resigned in 1996.

In the service of President Boris Yeltsin (1996-1999)

In August 1996, he was appointed Moscow deputy to Pavel Borodin, director of the Department of Presidential Property Administration (Russian: *Управление делами Президента Российской Федерации*). In March 1997, he joined the presidential administration *(Администрация Президента Российской Федерации)* to become deputy head, and at the same time becomes in charge of the Main Control Department *(Главное контрольное управление президента Российской Федерации)*. This department is accused by some of being a "mini-KGB" routinely making use of *kompromat*. Vladimir Putin then became (from May 1998) deputy director of the presidential administration in charge of managing relations with the regions, still with significant influence within the government. In July 1998, he was appointed Director of the Federal Security Service of the Russian Federation (FSB), a post he held for just over a year, until his appointment as Prime Minister on August 9, 1999. At the same time, from March to August 1999, he was Secretary of the Russian Security Council *(Совет безопасности Российской Федерации)*.

At this time, Boris Yeltsin was facing many difficulties: Yuri Skuratov, the Prosecutor General of the Russian Federation, was investigating assets in Switzerland belonging to him and his family, which had been used to buy luxury goods. On March 18, 1999, television broadcast a sulphurous video showing a man resembling Skouratov having sexual relations with two young women. He denied being the man in question, but Vladimir Putin announced in a television interview that his experts had definitively established that it was Skouratov. Skouratov was replaced by Vladimir Oustinov. According to the German media *Correctiv*, this scandal was invented by

Vladimir Putin and enabled him to get his hands on the Russian judicial system.

Boris Yeltsin's succession (1999)

In 1999, following the Russian financial crisis of 1998, Vladimir Putin's meteoric rise to power began. In August, he was appointed Prime Minister by Boris Yeltsin, replacing Sergei Stepashin, who had been appointed to the post on May 9. He thus became the second-in-command of the state, and his appointment was seen in Europe as the designation of Yeltsin's successor. The German media *Correctiv* sees this appointment as a gesture of gratitude from Boris Yeltsin to Vladimir Putin for having thwarted the Prosecutor General's investigation into him.

On November 14, 1999, Vladimir Putin authorized the General Prosecutor's Office of the Russian Federation to borrow $30 million from a foreign bank for the purchase of a new computer network: Hewlett-Packard (HP) was awarded the contract in February 2001, although its bid was not the cheapest. In return, HP paid 7.6 million euros in bribes to Russian officials, including prosecutors and secret service agents, enabling Vladimir Putin to consolidate his domination of the Russian judiciary. This transaction is covered by an export guarantee from Euler Hermes, which belongs to the German Allianz Group, and has been approved by the German Ministry of Economics and Labor.

In early September 1999, attacks on apartment buildings in Moscow and other Russian cities claimed several hundred victims, and were attributed by Russian judicial authorities to Chechen terrorists from the Islamist "Kavkaz" center. The official version of the origin of the attacks remains contested by opponents of Vladimir Putin: the few politicians and journalists to have looked into the September 1999 attacks have been imprisoned or, in most cases, murdered, such as former spy Alexander Litvinenko and journalist Anna Politkovskaya. Having been hostile to the first Chechen war, Russian public opinion is hoping for new military operations to put an end to the Chechen separatists.

At a press conference in Kazakhstan's new capital, Astana, at the end of September 1999, Vladimir Putin declared that the terrorists would have to be "flushed down the toilet".

With the support of President Yeltsin and the General Staff, Putin issued an ultimatum to resume hostilities in Chechnya in order to "restore federal constitutional order". The second Chechen war (officially called the "anti-terrorist operation") began on October 1er 1999. At the start of his term of office, he was credited with just

3% of the presidential vote, far behind Primakov, but the number of votes cast in his favor increased considerably.

President of the Russian Federation

First presidential term (2000-2004)

On December 31, 1999, following the surprise resignation of Boris Yeltsin, Putin, in his capacity as Prime Minister, became acting President. His first official act was to sign a presidential decree granting his predecessor total immunity from all possible legal proceedings involving him and members of his family.

Vladimir Putin was officially elected President of the Russian Federation on March 26, 2000, in the first round of the early presidential election, with 52.94% of the vote against 29.21% for Gennady Zyuganov (Communist Party) and 5.80% for Grigory Yavlinsky (Yabloko Party). As for the other nine candidates, each received less than 3% of the vote.

Aged 47, he officially took office for his first term on May 7, 2000. He sees himself as Russia's savior, and claims to want to restore the country's power and grandeur, imposing authoritarian methods from the outset.

In September 2000, an account of Vladimir Putin's election campaign, based on six months' investigative work and published in the *Moscow Times*, uncovered evidence of electoral fraud, including ballot box stuffing and destruction and a million three hundred thousand "dead souls" on the electoral rolls. For Noam Chomsky and Edward Herman, "his electoral success rested largely on the fact that the powerful state radio and television stations campaigned furiously in his favor, denigrating and denying airtime to his opponents".

Second presidential term (2004-2008)

In March 2004, he was again re-elected as President of the Russian Federation in the first round, with 71.22% of the vote. The Communist Party candidate Nikolai Kharitonov received only 13.69% of the vote, with the rest of the candidates receiving less than 5%.

Vertical power

Vladimir Putin, determined to restore what he calls "the vertical of power", governs with a style considered by some analysts to be authoritarian, which would have put an end to the political liberalization introduced by Gorbachev with *perestroika* and *glasnost* and which had continued under Boris Yeltsin, with some Western media and political opponents speaking of him as neo-tsarism.

The Putin administration's return to control of the country, after the period of unrest and laissez-faire that prevailed under Boris Yeltsin, satisfies a large part of the population, weary of the political upheavals and transitional capitalism ("shock therapy") that emerged after the fall of communism, as well as those nostalgic for the power of the former Soviet Union, which disappeared in 1991. This takeover also responds to the risk to the unity of the Russian Federation posed by the rise of nationalism in ethnically non-Russian republics and increasingly autonomous local governors: the weakening of central power and the economic and social collapse following the demise of the Soviet Union forced Russia's major regions to seek self-government in the 1990s.

During his two terms in office, President Putin steadily strengthened the influence of the intelligence services from which he emerged, as well as the police and army, known in Russian as the *Siloviki* (*men of strength*), as opposed to the liberals, supporters of the rule of law and Western-style democracy . In fact, according to political scientist Vyacheslav Aviutskii, the "Guebists" (FSB (ex-KGB) cadres) temporarily lost influence during the Yeltsin period, when he remained very suspicious of the KGB, but returned in force under Putin. According to him, they used a rather soft reformer, Mikhail Gorbachev, to destroy a system that had simply become ineffective. The Guebists saw themselves as the only moral force capable of stemming the corruption that had spread throughout the Soviet leadership. In their eyes, power had to remain in the hands of the military, in the broadest sense, and in those of national security". The *siloviki* see themselves above all as patriots concerned with the recovery and development of their country, as opposed to the Western-backed oligarchs, driven above all by the desire to build a personal fortune on the rubble of the Soviet Union, with little regard for the means to achieve it. In reality, cases of prevarication and corruption also concern representatives of the "organs". The latter, along with influential figures from St. Petersburg (the *piterskiye*), Putin's hometown (and also the most "European" of Russia's major cities), are now well represented in presidential politics and administration. Together, they form, writes Macha Lipman, analyst at the Carnegie Endowment for International Peace, "a closed vertical system". Vladimir Putin's sponsorship of Dmitri Medvedev as Head of State (winner of the March 2008 presidential election), a jurist with a liberal reputation and no background in *siloviki*, suggests, however, that this political system retains a certain degree of openness.

In addition to greater stability, a number of Western leaders appreciate the fact that Vladimir Putin has fostered an economy that has returned to growth, favoring trade and major contracts.

Managing the oligarch issue

Right from the start of his presidential term, Vladimir Putin was determined to establish a "dictatorship of law" and to combat the parastatal mafia and tax evasion of the industrial and financial oligarchs, whose stranglehold on the Russian economy was becoming a major concern for the population after an era of laissez-faire and Boris Yeltsin's complicity in the creation of this oligarchy.

- Several oligarchs who had monopolized resources and industrial assets, taking advantage of the loopholes in the transitional business law, were brought to heel or prosecuted (e.g. banker Sergei Mavrodi). The emblematic example is that of Mikhail Khodorkovsky, ex-chief executive of the Yukos oil group, sentenced to eight years in prison for fraud and large-scale tax evasion, and imprisoned in Siberia. The Yukos group dates back to the Soviet era. It was acquired under dubious conditions by Khodorkovsky in the mid-1990s, for a mere $309 million, as part of privatizations dubbed the "hold-up of the century". By 2003, following the acquisition of Sibneft, Yukos had become Russia's leading oil company and the fourth largest in the world. It seems that it was the plan to sell the Yukos group to a North American oil company for $40 billion that triggered the campaign against Khodorkovsky. Negotiations were underway with Exxon-Mobil and Chevron-Texacos with a view to a partial merger with Yukos-Sibneft, and it seems that Khodorkovsky had also established contacts with Halliburton, the energy company headed by Dick Cheney until 2000. According to the Vedomosti agency, observers believe that Putin could see Mikhail Khodorkovsky as a political adversary: "The authorities fear an early release of Mr. Khodorkovsky, a worsening of the domestic political situation in the run-up to the elections and, of course, an increase in the number of foreign trials", adds Igor Yurgens, Vice-President of the Russian Union of Industrialists and Entrepreneurs.

- Others seem to enjoy a certain impunity, such as Pavel Fedoulev who, in September 2000, seized the Uralkhimmash metallurgical combine with the help of OMON (the Ministry of the Interior's special forces). The long series of contested privatizations in the Russian metallurgical industry, which began in 1991, continues under President Putin's government.

The ousting of several oligarchs from the media they owned (Berezovsky, Gusinsky and a few others) strengthened state control over mass information and induced a de facto censorship harmful to political pluralism in Russia, reinforced by indirect pressure on the rest of the independent press' . However, alongside broad public support for Vladimir Putin, and despite the omnipresence of a media apparatus that is sometimes considered parastatal, there are declared opponents of the president's policies in Russia, and a fraction of the media retains a critical eye (including outlets such as *Kommersant*, which is now part of the Gazprom galaxy). But freedom of tone remains rather partial, as evidenced by the dismissal at the end of 2011 of two of Kommersant's editorial directors by the oligarch Alisher Usmanov.

Economic and social policy

A major series of reforms

Right from the start of his mandate, Vladimir Putin embarked on major socio-economic and political reforms that have significantly transformed Russia.

In the economic field :

- tax reform: introduction of a single income tax rate of 13%, introduction of a unified social security tax, reduction in the VAT rate, reduction in the corporate tax rate from 35% to 24%, simplifying taxation and limiting fraud and corruption;

- land reform introducing the right to sell agricultural land;

- four state deregulation laws aimed at reducing bureaucratic control of companies;

- opening up rail freight, which accounts for 80% of the country's freight traffic, to competition.

In the social sector :

- pension reform: introduction of a three-pillar system with compulsory capitalization and voluntary savings, without increasing the retirement age;

- implementation of the National Priority Projects and Population Policy to reform the social sector and finance major projects in the fields of health, education, accessibility of social housing, support for the agricultural sector and increasing the birth rate.

In the political sphere, reforms have focused on creating a "power vertical" to make power more concentrated and efficient (this process was accelerated following the Beslan tragedy on September 1er 2004):

- reform of the territorial division with the creation of seven Federal Districts by Presidential Decree no.° 849 of May 13, 2000;

- reform of the Council of the Russian Federation (2000-2002), and the end of elections of governors by the subjects of the federation: district governors are now appointed by the country's president (Kremlin) with subsequent ratification by local legislation (September 2004);

- creation of advisory bodies: a State Council (Gossoviet), made up of governors, and a

Chamber of Society (Obshchestvennaia Palata), made up of influential and well-known personalities;

- measures to ensure greater cohesion between the so-called *siloviki* ministries of public order (Interior, Army, FSB) and the Ministry of Emergency Situations.

According to the government, the success of these reforms, coupled with extraordinary tax revenues from the sale of hydrocarbons, has led to a substantial rise in real personal income (+58.5% between 1999 and 2002, +13.55% in 2004). This has earned Putin the support of a large part of the Russian population, despite a few setbacks, such as a controversial bill on the monetization of benefits in kind inherited from the Soviet era, which caused a public outcry in early 2005, or the sinking of the Kursk K-141 submarine in 2000 with 118 crewmen on board, and the difficult liberation of the Chechen commando hostages from the Moscow theater in October 2002.

Continued policy of rapprochement with the West

Putin's foreign policy during his first term was a continuation of Yeltsin's policy. He went even further, proposing to the EU the creation of a single economic market and to the United States Russia's entry into NATO, but the United States refused both offers. Putin's accession to power was formally decided by Boris Yeltsin. It came about thanks to the rapid military resolution of a particularly deadly conflict in the Russian republic of Chechnya, and was bolstered by a voluntarist rhetoric calling for the restoration of the state, the fight against corruption (far from complete by the end of 2007) and the revival, at least in part, of the prestige of a fallen superpower in the eyes of the Russians.

This foreign policy was intended as a counterpart to a domestic policy aimed at combating the decomposition of the country following the political, economic and social collapse of 1991 (between 1991 and 1996, Russian GNP collapsed by 40%).

Following NATO's Operation Allied Force intervention in the Federal Republic of Yugoslavia in 1999, which was perceived as an act of aggression by the Russian leadership, a new military doctrine was drawn up: following the example of the United States' military doctrine, the use of nuclear weapons for tactical purposes on the battlefield was authorized; according to this doctrine, the strengthening of the Russian military apparatus should serve the geostrategic interests of the state without concern for "Western considerations".

The terrorist attack of September 11, 2001 transformed, for a time, the geostrategic situation for Russia and gave impetus to the establishment of closer relations with the United States. Putin's open support for his American counterpart in his "fight against terrorism" initially established a climate of a certain cordiality and a new understanding between the two powers. A pragmatic and realistic perception of international issues, on both the Russian and American sides, enabled Russia to make a strong comeback on the international stage, playing a predominant role in the fight against terrorism or being involved in mediation efforts in complex issues such as the Israeli-Palestinian conflict, North Korea or Iran.

At the beginning of 2007, faced with plans to install American ballistic weapons systems in Poland and the Czech Republic (presented by the USA as a "shield", an anti-missile protection against possible Iranian nuclear attacks, but which *de facto* weaken Russia's nuclear deterrent against the American arsenal and are perceived as a threat by the Russian population), Putin raised the tone of his relations with the USA and NATO. In his speech to the Munich Security Conference on February 10, 2007, he expressly criticized the move of NATO bases closer to Russia's borders, in violation of the promises made to Gorbachev in the early 1990s, as well as a unipolar world with "Washington at the center", imposing its domestic laws and worldview on the entire international community. On June 4, 2007, on the eve of the G8 summit in Rostock, Vladimir Putin threatened to point

new Iskander missiles at Eastern Europe (a deployment
that would be accompanied by the installation of nuclear
weapons in the Russian enclave of Kaliningrad) if the
United States deployed its ballistic weapons on Russia's
borders, thus taking up at the highest level the veiled
threats previously expressed by Russian army chiefs.

Faced with the changes in the geostrategic situation in
Europe brought about by the United States, Russia
suspended the application of the Treaty on Conventional
Forces in Europe on December 12, 2007, creating a stir
within NATO and in Washington.

At the NATO summit in Bucharest in April 2008, when
invited to discuss the authorization of logistical transport
of non-military equipment on Russian soil, Vladimir Putin
declared that NATO's enlargement to include the former
Soviet republics of Ukraine and Georgia posed a threat to
Russia. Speaking of Ukraine, he made it clear that NATO
membership would not guarantee the country's
democratization.

Head of Medvedev's government (2008-2012)

As he nears the end of his second presidential term,
Vladimir Putin has repeatedly stated that he has no
intention of seeking a constitutional amendment to run
for a third consecutive term in March 2008.

He then announced his intention to lead the United Russia party's December 2007 election campaign for the presidency of the government, which would enable him to retain a degree of power while respecting the Constitution. On December 2, 2007, United Russia won the parliamentary elections with 64% of the vote. The 2007 elections were the first to be held in Russia on a fully proportional basis. This victory gave Vladimir Putin a "moral right", in his own words, to continue governing.

On December 10, 2007, Vladimir Putin officially endorsed Dmitri Medvedev to replace him as President. On the same day, Medvedev became the candidate for the 2008 presidential election nominated by four parties: United Russia, Just Russia, the Agrarian Party and Civil Force. Dmitri Medvedev, winner of the Russian presidential election on March 2, 2008, asked Vladimir Putin to assume the post of Prime Minister after his departure from the Kremlin. Medvedev was sworn in as head of government on May 7, 2008, the day his presidential term came to an end. On May 8, 2008, the State Duma ratified Vladimir Putin's appointment as head of government.

Vladimir Putin also agreed to head United Russia at its congress on April 15, 2008, but did not join.

Economic crisis of 2008

According to the World Bank, the crisis in Russia began in the private sector, triggering three shocks: the decline in domestic trade, the reflux of capital and the freeze on borrowing. The first signs of the crisis appeared in May 2008, when the Russian stock market began a downward trend and collapsed at the end of July. In addition, the Russian-Georgian conflict in August 2008, with the Americans offering lukewarm support to the Georgians, triggered a flight of capital out of Russia. It was in September-October that the first government measures were taken to strengthen the Russian financial system, following the example of other Western countries: recapitalization of banks, limiting the liquidity deficit of banks in particular, thus avoiding bankruptcy. [er]On October 1, 2008, Vladimir Putin declared that responsibility for the crisis lay with the US government and system, stressing that "everything that is happening today in the economic and financial sphere began, as we all know, in the United States".

On October 31, 2008, the head of government announced budget cuts for state monopolies and that further support for business would have to be provided without additional expenditure from the state budget. On November 8, 2008, he endorsed the President's measures for the financial sector and other sectors affected by the crisis. Import taxes on certain agricultural products were temporarily raised to support Russian agriculture, with effect from December 11, 2008. On December 19, 2008, the automotive sector was helped by the facilitation of credit for vehicle purchases and the provision of production financing. Capital outflows for 2008-2009 are estimated at $191.1 billion. On December 5, 2008, customs tariffs were raised in the automotive sector for foreign-brand light and heavy vehicles, provoking protests in Russia's Far Eastern provinces, which import Asian automobiles.

In November 2009, Vladimir Putin made an official visit to Paris, during which the partnership between France and Russia led to the signing of numerous trade agreements in the energy, defense and automotive sectors.

In March 2010, the World Bank reported that Russian losses had been lower than expected at the start of the crisis. Growth in the first quarter of 2010 was 2.9%, and the industrial sector grew by 5.8%, making Russia second only to Japan in the group of eight industrialized countries. However, during the first quarter of 2010, tens of thousands of people defied bans on demonstrations, first in Kaliningrad and then in some fifty cities, calling for Putin's resignation because of the rising cost of living" .

Contested bid for a third presidential term

On September 24, 2011, at the United Russia congress, President Dmitry Medvedev proposed Vladimir Putin as a candidate for the presidential election on March 4, 2012. On the same day, Putin confirmed his candidacy on the podium, with Dmitri Medvedev expected to take over as head of government after his victory. Vladimir Putin was officially sworn in as United Russia's candidate on November 27, 2011. He had been barred from standing for re-election in 2008, as the Russian Constitution imposed a limit of two consecutive terms; in addition, a constitutional reform in the meantime extended the presidential term from four to six years, which would allow him to remain in office until 2024. Following this announcement, Finance Minister Alexei Kudrin, who had long been considered for the post of government president in the event of Putin's candidacy, publicly criticized the decision, leading him to resign on September 26, 2011.

In the December 2011 parliamentary elections, United Russia won 49.32% of the vote, 15 points less than in 2007. According to observers, this was partly due to what was described as Medvedev's "sleight of hand". The elections were quickly contested because of alleged fraud in favor of the ruling party. As large-scale demonstrations took place calling for the election to be annulled, Putin's popularity rating fell to between 42% and 51% of those polled .

Although Putin remains the clear favorite in the race for the Kremlin, he is a contested leader among some sections of the population. Several anti-Putin demonstrations have taken place in Moscow and the country's major cities, mobilizing several thousand or even tens of thousands of people.

Third presidential term (2012-2018)

On March 4, 2012, Vladimir Putin was elected for a six-year term with 63.6% of the vote in the first round. Although the result was contested by the opposition, several heads of state, including Chinese President Hu Jintao, congratulated the president-elect. On the evening of the election, a concert in support of the President was organized in front of the Kremlin.

Putin's presidential inauguration took place on May 7, 2012, at an official ceremony in the Kremlin. On the same day, the new President of the Federation nominated his predecessor, Dmitry Medvedev, as President of the Government; the decision was considered and approved by Parliament.

On December 12, Vladimir Putin delivered his first address to the nation since his election to the presidency in the Kremlin banquet hall. During this lengthy speech, the Russian head of state made a large number of announcements, including the forthcoming creation of a tax on large fortunes, one of many reforms that Putin would like to implement to combat the illegal operations increasingly common in the Russian economy.

In 2013, Putin's skilful handling of the Edward Snowden eavesdropping affair, followed by his diplomatic maneuvering around Syria to avert an imminent Western military operation, demonstrated, according to political observers, Russia's growing importance and role on the international political stage. The arrival of the Olympic Games in Sochi the following year also increased media pressure on Russia.

At the same time, drawing on the traditional Christian and family values to which the Russian population is still largely faithful, Vladimir Putin criticizes the legalization of same-sex marriage in several Western countries. At his instigation, a law prohibiting "homosexual propaganda aimed at minors" was introduced. However, President Putin repeatedly pointed out that homosexuality had been decriminalized in Russia since 1991, and that discrimination based on sexual orientation was not legal. Several journalists criticized his links with the head of the republic of Chechnya - a member of Putin's United Russia party - Ramzan Kadyrov, who is accused of ordering several murders and inciting violence and torture against homosexuals, who are imprisoned and beaten in camps.

In December 2013, he dissolved the official news agency RIA Novosti to create a new organization, Rossia Segodnia. Through various channels, including the Sputnik news agency and RT cable TV, this new organization broadcasts a largely pro-Russian viewpoint abroad, not only on internal Russian affairs, but also specific to other countries.

Opponent Boris Nemtsov, who was about to publish a report entitled *Putin. War*, was assassinated in 2015 in front of the Kremlin, once again bringing people to the streets. The report dealt with Russia's invasion of Crimea, illegal under international law, and the Russian government's role in Ukraine's Donbass war, arming rebels in the east of the country. These actions, which the members of the Group of Eight consider to be warmongering, have led to Russia's suspension from the economic circle.

From the start of the Syrian civil war, Russia has been providing military support to the Syrian regime. On September 30, 2015, at the request of Bashar al-Assad, weakened by several setbacks, Russia intervened directly in Syria. The Russian air force then began a campaign of air strikes against the rebels and the Islamic State. On November 24, 2015, a Russian Sukhoi Su-24 was shot down by the Turkish air force near Latakia and a pilot killed, causing a diplomatic crisis between Russia and Turkey, until their reconciliation in the summer of 2016. However, the Russians' intervention tipped the balance in favor of the loyalists, who once again made progress on several fronts. Negotiations are held between the United

States and Russia in an attempt to achieve a ceasefire between the rebels and the regime and a political settlement to the conflict. Truces were declared in Syria in January and September 2016, but each lasted only a few days' . At the end of 2016, Russian and Iranian military intervention led to a victory for the loyalist camp in the Battle of Aleppo. However, Russian and Syrian bombing caused the deaths of several thousand civilians in rebel neighborhoods; hospitals and Syrian civil defense barracks were repeatedly targeted until they were completely destroyed. The Russian air force also uses "Bunker buster" bombs, cluster bombs and incendiary bombs'''' . In autumn 2016, the Syrian regime and Russia were accused of war crimes by the United States, France, the United Kingdom, the European Union and Amnesty International'' . Jean-Marc Ayrault condemned Russia's "strategy of total war", while Boris Johnson felt that "the international community has a duty to protect" the Syrian people in the face of the "horror" of Russian strikes. He also told the British Parliament that "if it means confronting Russian air power [...], then it must be done".

Vladimir Putin announces the creation of a 400,000-strong National Guard, which will replace the traditional army and be tasked with protecting institutions and maintaining order in the event of major domestic unrest.

His term of office was marked by a wave of support from Europe's far-right parties, as well as from some left-wing and far-left parties.

On October 27, 2016, the Russian president made a speech in Sochi, refuting claims by Barack Obama and Hillary Clinton that Russian hackers at his behest were responsible for the hacking of US Democratic Party databases. However, the US President relies on preliminary research initiated by the Federal Bureau of Investigation, pointing in this direction. Putin is neutral on the outcome of the 2016 US presidential election between Donald Trump and Hillary Clinton. He would, however, have a slight preference for a Trump victory, which he believes would defend the interests of "ordinary" people in the United States' .

In June 2017, US pay-TV channel Showtime broadcast a documentary by American director Oliver Stone, *The Putin Interviews*, in which the Kremlin leader warns of renewed hostility between the US and Russia, and declares his belief that "no one would survive an episode of armed conflict" between the two countries. He added that, despite current tensions, he "did not despair of a restoration of relations with Washington". Reacting to the upheaval caused by the Russiagate affair, he said that former FBI director James Comey had "provided no

evidence that Russia interfered in the U.S. election"
during his Senate testimony.

Fourth presidential term (since 2018)

Vladimir Putin ran for another term in the 2018
presidential election, which he won in the first round. As
in previous elections, the main opponents were unable to
take part, and electoral fraud and irregularities marred
the ballot, although the extent of these is not easy to
assess' . He was sworn in for his new term as President of
Russia on May 7, 2018. On the same day, he proposed the
reappointment of Medvedev as head of government.

In October 2018, his popularity reached one of its lowest
levels, mainly due to a highly unpopular reform involving
a five-year increase in the retirement age.

On January 15, 2020, Vladimir Putin proposed a reform of
the Russian Constitution, strengthening the powers of
Parliament at the expense of presidential power. On
February 14, he announced an amendment to the
Constitution, with the aim of mentioning "God" and
stating that marriage is possible "only between a man and
a woman". On March 10, 2020, the Duma votes on an
amendment to the draft constitutional revision that
would allow Vladimir Putin and former president Dmitry
Medvedev to run for two consecutive terms after 2024,
paving the way for the Russian president to remain in

power until 2036. On March 14, Vladimir Putin signed a constitutional amendment allowing him to run for two more terms. After validation of the text by the Constitutional Court, the President announced that a referendum vote would be held on April 22 if the "health situation" - linked to the Covid-19 pandemic - allowed it. This was not the case, and Vladimir Putin announced on June 1er 2020 that the referendum would be held at the beginning of the following month' . On July 1er 2020, the constitutional revision was adopted with 77.9% of the votes cast. On July 21, Vladimir Putin signed a decree giving the country until 2030 to halve poverty, with the aim of completing "Russia's development goals" by that date. On December 22, he passed a law granting lifelong immunity from prosecution to former presidents and their relatives: the new law stipulates that a former Russian president "cannot be prosecuted criminally or administratively"; nor can he be arrested by the police, interrogated or searched.

In November, Vladimir Putin plays a key role in obtaining a ceasefire declaration, putting an end to the war in Nagorno-Karabakh.

In a video published on YouTube on January 19, 2021, which he presents as the result of an investigation carried out by his Anti-Corruption Foundation (FBK), opponent Alexeï Navalny denounces the lavishness and financing of

"Putin's palace", a huge mansion with numerous amenities (heliport, skating rink, casino, swimming pool, spa, aquadiscotheque, etc.). Among other things, the opponent claims that President Putin has a "pathological" taste for luxury, and details financial arrangements designed to "create a buffer around the palace" from its true owner. Three days after its publication, the nearly two-hour video had been viewed more than 53 million times. Kremlin spokesman Dmitry Peskov reacted by claiming not to have seen it, but at the same time indicating that nothing she said was true᾽. Demonstrations broke out across the country in support of Navalny, imprisoned since his return to Russia on January 13, and against President Vladimir Putin, who was accused of being a "thief" by the demonstrators. In response, Vladimir Putin accused the West of using Navalny to "try to contain Russia".

On May 20, 2021, at a meeting on Russia's latest defensive weapons, including the Avangard super-missile, Vladimir Putin said that many Western powers "do not accept the vastness of Russia". However, Moscow welcomed "positive signals" in the progress of Russian-American relations, with Washington announcing the lifting of certain sanctions against the strategic Nord Stream 2 gas pipeline.

On June 4, 2021, Vladimir Putin promulgated a law, adopted in May by the Duma, prohibiting employees of organizations classified by the courts as "extremist" from taking part in elections. A large part of the opposition sees this as a way of limiting the number of candidates hostile to the current government.

The presidential party, United Russia, leads the 2021 parliamentary elections with 49.8% of the votes cast. Without supporting evidence, the opposition accuses the government of electoral fraud, speaking of "ballot box stuffing" and "online vote manipulation". The European Union denounced a "climate of intimidation", the United States felt that "Russians have been prevented from exercising their civil rights" and the United Kingdom deplored a "serious setback for democratic freedoms". For his part, Vladimir Putin thanked the Russians for "their confidence" following this victory, which strengthened him with a new majority in the Duma, two years before the presidential election of 2024.

Invasion of Ukraine

In February 2022, he officially recognized the separatist republics of Donetsk and Lugansk, while relations with Ukraine had been tense for several months. In the early hours of February 24, Vladimir Putin makes a speech announcing the launch of Russia's invasion of Ukraine with the aim of "demilitarizing and denazifying" the country, describing the attack as a "military operation". Within minutes of this declaration, the armed forces of the Russian Federation entered Ukrainian territory. Throughout the first day, almost all the member countries of the European Union, the United States and the UN, in resolution ES-11/1, unanimously condemned the Russian invasion of Ukraine, and announced economic sanctions and military reinforcements in support of the Ukrainian armed forces. US President Joe Biden declared that he would "not send troops to Ukrainian soil", but that he would "defend every inch of NATO territory". Emmanuel Macron, President of the French Republic, said in an address that "Vladimir Putin has broken his word" and affirmed that "France stands by the Ukrainian people". British Prime Minister Boris Johnson and US President Joe Biden described the Russian president as a "dictator", condemning the Russian offensive"" . On February 25,

2022, Vladimir Putin was placed on the European Union's blacklist.

On September 9, 2022, following a Russian military setback in the invasion of Ukraine, two groups of municipal deputies in St. Petersburg and Moscow called for the impeachment of Vladimir Putin, with no chance of success. According to former MI6 agent Christopher Steele, Putin would not survive a defeat in Ukraine. On September 21, 2022, Vladimir Putin announced a partial mobilization of 300,000 reservists and renewed the nuclear threat "if Russia's interests are threatened". On September 30, Vladimir Putin's Russia annexed four occupied regions in southern and eastern Ukraine (the Luhansk, Donetsk, Zaporijjia and Kherson oblasts), where fighting is still going on and its army does not have full control.

Privacy policy

In 1982, Putin met Lyudmila Alexandrovna Chkrebneva, a young flight attendant, whom he married the following year. They have two daughters, Maria, born in 1985 in Leningrad, and Ekaterina, born in 1986 in Dresden.

On June 6, 2013, confirming the many rumors of their separation that they had repeatedly denied, Vladimir and Lyudmila Putin announced their divorce in an interview with the *Rossiya 24* channel' .

Putin, still married, is said to have had an affair with Svetlana Krivonogikh (en), a former cleaning lady who suddenly became a millionaire after the birth of their daughter Elizaveta in 2003' . He then became involved with gymnast Alina Kabaeva, thirty years his junior, whom he helped to get elected to the State Duma in 2007, and with whom he had three children. The number of children may in fact be four: two boys and two twin girls. All four children were born in Switzerland and hold Swiss passports.

Through Maria Vorontsova, Vladimir Putin is the grandfather of two grandsons born in 2015 and 2017' , and, through Katerina Tikhonova, of a granddaughter born in 2017.

In April 2022, following the Boutcha massacre in Ukraine, Maria Vorontsova and Katerina Tikhonova, his daughters from his first marriage to Lyudmila Alexandrovna Chkrebneva, were sanctioned by the United States, the European Union and the United Kingdom' .

Vladimir Putin owns several dogs.

Position statements

Economy

In 1999, he announced his intention to structure the Russian economy through a network of SMEs: "The State must act where and when it is needed; freedom must exist where and when it is required". According to journalist Frédéric Pons, Vladimir Putin is an "economic liberal". During his first two presidential terms, Putin surrounded himself with liberal ministers and advisors, including Andrei Illarionov.

However, Morozov believes that Vladimir Putin cannot be described as a liberal either in economic terms - "at the time, he adopted a neutral economic form, common in the West, neither left-wing nor liberal in the classical sense" - or in political terms - "having developed his views within the KGB, he initiated a policy that had absolutely nothing to do with liberalism"; he sums up Vladimir Putin's project in the desire to "build an effective, contemporary imperial system based on a market economy". For Alexander Morozov, "at that time, he was not promoting a specific 'Russian way', but a thoroughly European political philosophy". More generally, he believes that "Putin's fundamental philosophy remains economic-centric. He wants to gain resources to participate in global capitalism with new forces. But he does not propose an alternative doctrine to global financial capitalism. He doesn't want to destroy it or propose anything else.

During its first two terms in office, the Russian government brought strategic economic sectors monopolized by oligarchs, notably hydrocarbons, back under state control. In 2001, a single income tax rate of 13% was introduced, and a new labor code more favorable to employers was adopted in 2002. The authorities added a compulsory funded system to the pension system; 6% of pension contributions were thus channelled not into financing current pensions, but into financial intermediaries or private pension funds.

In 2005, following a protest movement unprecedented since the early 1990s, the government was forced to introduce a number of social reforms, including the strengthening of family allowances. Following the economic crisis of 2008, and the sanctions imposed by the United States and the European Union in 2014, which plunged Russia into recession, the government relaunched its austerity policy, cutting back on certain social spending. On the tax front, the authorities opted to increase taxes on labor (by raising income tax and VAT rates) and reduce taxes on capital. Numerous subsidies and tax credits are granted to large companies, including the most profitable. According to the State Audit Office, these tax breaks have resulted in a shortfall of 11,000 billion rubles (145 billion euros) for the State budget.

Attitude towards the USSR

As soon as he became president, Vladimir Putin reinstated the Soviet Union's anthem, against the opinion of a significant part of his administration, by changing the lyrics. In 2005, he declared that the "disintegration of the USSR was the greatest geopolitical catastrophe of the XXe century", but also: "Whoever does not regret the dissolution of the Soviet Union has no heart; whoever wants to resurrect the Soviet Union has no brain". In his speech on March 18, 2014, delivered on the occasion of the annexation of Crimea, he persisted: "What seemed unthinkable, unfortunately, has become real. The USSR has disintegrated", thus supporting the reconquest of the former Soviet territory.

In January 2016, he accused Lenin of having "blown up Russia": "Ideas must lead to good results, not as they did with Vladimir Ilyich". An advocate of a strong state, he criticized Lenin for imposing the federalism that led to the break-up of the country over 80 years later.

According to Alexander Morozov, editor-in-chief of the online daily *Russki Journal*, the "cognitive pattern of late Sovietism is evident in its approach to the West, its contempt for international organizations, and its contemptuous attitude towards Russia's neighboring 'little peoples'".

On February 21, 2022, in a speech on the recognition of the Donetsk and Lugansk People's Republics as part of the Ukrainian Crisis, Putin asserts that "Ukraine was entirely built and created by Lenin", that "The Communist Party created Ukraine [...] and Khrushchev gave Crimea for certain reasons [...]" and that "It was a mistake to grant exit rights from the USSR to the Soviet republics".

Slavophilism

Also inspired by Ivan Iline, Vladimir Putin is resolutely Slavophile after his return to the presidency in 2012. In his victory speech, he declared: "The policy of containing Russia, which continued in the XVIIIe century, the XIXe century and the XXe century, continues today. People are always trying to push us back into a corner because we have an independent position". Aleksandr Morozov points out that since then, Vladimir Putin has used the terms "Russian civilization" and "civilizational code". Aleksandr Prokhanov, a far-right, anti-Western Russian journalist and writer, considered in 2014 that his ideas were "beginning to take effect" among Vladimir Putin's advisors, and that he was "restoring to its original imperial form the state scuttled by Boris Yeltsin after the collapse of the USSR".

Conservatism

Journalists Vincent Jauvert and Frédéric Pons disagree that Vladimir Putin strengthened his conservative stance after his return to the presidency in 2012. On December 12, 2013, Vladimir Putin called, before all the nation's representatives, for the "defense of traditional values", and described his stance as "conservative". He also regularly draws on the thought of Ivan Iline, whose remains he has had repatriated. With this in mind, the Russian government has set up "Institutes for Democracy and Cooperation" in New York and Paris. After initial contacts with the Orthodox Church via anti-abortion groups in Europe, it is also forging close links with right-wing populist movements, including the Front National in France, notably, according to *Le Nouvel Observateur*, with a view to "destabilizing the European political scene" and "weakening the transatlantic link".

At the 2019 G20 summit, Vladimir Putin declares that "liberalism is obsolete" and that liberal values come "into conflict with the interests of the overwhelming majority of the population", developing his point in particular on the subject of migrants .

Eurasism

In the late 1990s, Vladimir Putin frequented a study circle devoted to Lev Goumilev, one of the last historical representatives of Eurasism. Although he tried to draw closer to NATO in the 2000s, notably proposing a grand alliance to the United States in the wake of the September 11, 2001 attacks, the integration of former Eastern Bloc countries into NATO forced him to abandon this intention, and explains his reaction to attempts to integrate Georgia and Ukraine into NATO. In his speech on December 12, 2013, he quotes Lev Goumilev, referring to his concept of the "passionarity" or "inner energy" of the Russian people, and calls the development of Siberia and the Russian Far East "a national priority for the entire 21st^e century". The "Eurasian Economic Union" project, due to be launched in 2015, is part of this approach. It also reflects Western Europe's lack of interest in his proposal for a "Europe from Lisbon to Vladivostok". For Frédéric Pons, "these immense markets offer Russia growth relays and interesting strategic depth". According to Alexandre Terletzski, "the new Tsar, as we like to call him, sees himself as the great defender of a multipolar world still rejected by the United States".

Climate

Vladimir Putin has a rather climate-skeptical stance. On the subject of global warming, for example, he has said: "No one can say for sure what the cause is". Given the Russian economy's heavy dependence on fossil fuel exports, the Russian president said of the European

Union's fossil fuel phase-out target: "By defending this kind of proposal, it seems to me that mankind can go back to living in caves because it will no longer consume anything". More recently, he was more concerned about the climate, declaring: "The scale and nature of natural disasters in some regions are absolutely unprecedented" and "All this shows once again how important it is for us to make a deep and systematic commitment to the climate and environmental agenda in the future". Russia is one of the signatories to the Paris climate agreement, which did table a new greenhouse gas emissions reduction plan for COP26, held in Glasgow in November 2021, but no more ambitious than previous ones. He believes that the energy transition is too brutal.

Popularity and influence

In Russia

His popularity rating reached almost 60% in 2008, at the height of the war with Georgia. In August 2011, it fell to 39%, but he remains the country's most popular politician, according to a survey by the Levada Analytical Center, which points out that "people tend to hold Medvedev responsible for the country's problems [whereas] Putin is seen more as the national leader who solves crises".

The annexation of Crimea markedly increased his confidence rating, which reached 87% in August 2014 according to Levada′ . In March 2016, according to a poll published in the *Washington Post*, 83% of Russians approved of his action. RTL explains this popularity by the "patriotism that drives the Russian Nation". According to RTL's analysis, he represents the return of the mighty Russia, imposing, strong and ruthless. He is like "a second father to them". He represents change and progress for them. That's why young people admire him so much. They see him as the torch that represents Russia in the eyes of the world, and which they can wave. As he himself said in his 2018 election campaign, "strong president [means] strong Russia". In a way, then, it's the imagery that Putin sends back to Russia that enables him to grow in popularity. Through his image as a strong, athletic man, he forged this charismatic, imposing persona. To make himself known and loved by all, he placed portraits and paintings of himself in schools, among other places. In this way, he was able to win over young people in particular. As for those who didn't admire him, he used fear to gain respect. Putin's imagery and history also tend to instill fear in the former KGB chief. This is particularly the case because some anti-Kremlin or anti-Putin citizens have been murdered, whether as a result of crimes organized by Russian intelligence services, as Sergey Markov believes, or by Putin himself, according to some opponents. In addition, many media outlets are subject to censorship, particularly social media, which serve as a means of dissemination for the opposition. In Russia, "the media remain heavily monitored by the state in a variety of ways", according to academic Tina Burrett.

At the start of Putin's political career, particularly after his election as President of Russia in 2000, he was admired by a large proportion of the population. In 2017, his popularity rating in Russia stood at around 85%. But in 2018, his popularity dropped by twenty points, mainly due to the disputed pension reform and falling purchasing power. After nearly 19 years at Russia's helm, Putin's popularity is beginning to decline. After years in power, despite challenges and conspiracy theories presented by the opposition, Vladimir Putin had so far managed to maintain a good standing in relation to Russian opinion. In 2019, he is undertaking reforms to raise the retirement age, which will not go down well with the public. The Levada Analytical Center reports that 40% of Russian citizens are dissatisfied with Putin. This means he has gone from 80% approval in February 2010 to 64% in February 2019.

In the rest of the world

In March 2015, according to a study by the Pew Research Center, the foreign countries that most favor Vladimir Putin are Vietnam (70%) and China (54%)' . In October 2015, following Russia's intervention in Syria, Vladimir Putin's popularity exploded in Iraq' . One way or another, Putin has succeeded in gaining respect in Russia. Nevertheless, to consolidate his image, he needs to present himself to the world. Putin has always been keen to preserve his image as a strong, independent man - in a word, a capable man. To preserve this trademark image, he needs to take control of certain situations. Vladimir Putin's image in the world is mixed. By taking a firm stance in a conflict or helping certain countries, Russia has succeeded in forging alliances and Putin in boosting his popularity. Thanks to Russia's intervention in Syria in

2015, Middle Eastern and/or communist countries saw Russia as an ally. Mohammed Karim Nihaya, an Iraqi painter asserts that "the Russians are getting results" unlike "the United States and its allies [who] have been bombing for a year without achieving anything". This situation, for example, is one of the phenomena contributing to the perception of Vladimir Putin as a man of action. Putin's popularity continues to grow in these countries, while it remains mixed in Europe and North America. As Nina Bachkatov puts it, Putin is "the man the West loves to hate".

Only 12% of Germans trust Vladimir Putin more than Angela Merkel, but 23% in the Länder that made up the former GDR. In France, a 2014 BVA poll showed that 84% of French people have a poor opinion of Vladimir Putin, and 14% a good one. According to Ifop, Vladimir Putin received 20% positive and 80% negative opinions among French people in 2013, and 27% positive and 73% negative opinions in 2018. He receives the most favorable opinions among sympathizers of the far left, the right and the far right . In 2017, Ifop indicated that 53% of French people polled preferred Vladimir Putin, compared with 25% who preferred Donald Trump.

According to a Gallup poll, his approval rating among US Republican voters tripled between 2015 and 2017.

Vladimir Putin has cultivated this strong image from the outset. He has based his political career on his image, using the cult of personality. Whether it's simple magazine appearances, where he's not presented as a powerful president, it's as an inveterate sportsman. From judo to karate to skiing, he always makes sure he looks heroic in public. In addition to his tough image, the various magazine covers featuring him have helped reinforce his image overseas.

He was *Time Magazine*'s Personality of the Year 2007. According to *Forbes'* list of the world's most powerful people, Vladimir Putin is the most powerful man in the world in 2013, 2014, 2015 and 2016. He is also the only personality to be continuously in the annual top 5 since the creation of this ranking in 2009. According to a 2012 Pew poll relayed by Foreign Policy, 72% of Russians support Putin and his policies.

Criticism and controversy

Governance and authoritarian drift

In addition to accusations of electoral fraud in the 2000, 2008, 2011' , 2012, 2016 and 2018 elections, some analysts consider that Vladimir Putin's power is drifting towards authoritarianism. In October 2006, Marie Mendras, a researcher at CERI and lecturer at the Institut d'études politiques de Paris, judged that in Russia, "there is no longer any Parliament or Constitutional Court worthy of the name, the government is bypassed by the presidential administration, and judges are subject to political power as soon as a case becomes delicate. Violence and impunity reign everywhere [...]. It's a reign of opaque decisions, arbitrariness and expeditious methods".

However, several public players and experts take a more favorable view. On January 18, 2007, former German Chancellor Gerhard Schröder, currently Chairman of the Supervisory Board of the German-Russian gas consortium *North-European Gas Pipeline Co* (51% owned by Gazprom), warned against "the typical errors made in the West's assessment of Russia and its President". In his view, "the Russian President has succeeded in substantially raising the country's standard of living and re-establishing the state", and has "the historic merit of having set Russia on the path to stability and reliability as a partner". Acknowledging that, in many areas, Russia "is only at the beginning of a long and difficult road", Gerhard Schröder invited Russia's opponents not to look for faults in its actions and shortcomings from the point of view of Western democracy, but to support its efforts as it moves towards democracy. "Certainly, Russia has shortcomings, but no one knows them better than Russia's leaders, and no one will be able to overcome them better than they," stressed the former Chancellor. Interviewed by the Huffington Post, journalist and historian Galia Ackerman asserts that "He helped stabilize the country, and that's absolutely true". While conceding that "the standard of living has risen sharply", she points out that "he took advantage of this to further improve the standard of living of civil servants and those in sectors close to the State, such as security and justice".

Vladimir Putin was named *Time*'s Personality of the Year in 2007, a controversial accolade due to the 2006 assassination in London of Alexander Litvinenko, which several British journalists and investigators blamed on Russian power. The title of *Time Magazine*'s online edition attempts to sum up the essence of the Russian president's domestic policy: "Choosing order before freedom". The arrest, trial and imprisonment of members of the militant feminist group Pussy Riot is given as an example.

For the newspaper *Vedomosti*, "the rising level of crime and the number of bizarre and strangely lenient verdicts only serve to reinforce the sense of injustice within Russian society". However, the rate of intentional homicide has fallen under Vladimir Putin's presidency . Under Boris Yeltsin, around 19 people per 100,000 inhabitants died a violent death, compared with 10.2 per 100,000 in 2010. Human rights associations, including Memorial in Russia, founded by Andrei Sakharov, and a minority of opponents believe that the rule of law is under threat in the country, and denounce media self-censorship. Several independent press titles, as well as the NTV television channel, have been bought up by Gazprom and other state-controlled structures, and appear to have reduced their critical eye.

From 2005 onwards, a section of the opposition came together on several occasions to organize demonstrations, such as the March of Disagreement, Strategy-31, Putin Must Go, in which, however, the most important opposition parties in the Duma (Communist Party, Rodina, LDPR), did not participate. This movement brings together a wide range of political currents, including liberals, the Other Russia and, until 2006, the

National-Bolshevik Party. Its leaders include chess champion Garry Kasparov, dissident Edward Limonov, former prime minister Mikhail Kasyanov, lawyer Alexei Navalny, activist Sergei Udaltsov and statesman Boris Nemtsov. These demonstrations are often banned for various reasons by the authorities, and activists are arrested, imprisoned or subjected to pressure[ ] . The candidacy of these opponents is frequently rejected for various reasons. Some notable anti-Putin activists have been assassinated, such as Yuri Chervochkin and Boris Nemtsov, while others have suffered assassination attempts, such as Vladimir Vladimirovich Kara-Murza[ ] .

While the fall of the USSR saw the advent of press freedom, Vladimir Putin's presidencies are said to have reintroduced certain forms of censorship - such as the works of artist Konstantin Altunin, who in 2013 exhibited a painting depicting Putin in women's underwear, causing the museum to close and Altunin to flee - and propaganda. The official channels broadcast a pronounced anti-American discourse, discrediting, according to Pierre Avril of Le *Figaro*, with the help of videos supplied by the secret services, the opponents of power, while the Kremlin, according to the same journalist, pays Internet users to post pro-Putin dithyrambic comments and attacks on members of the opposition. Numerous journalists critical of the regime and its president have been assassinated, without their murders being clearly elucidated, such as Paul Klebnikov, Anna Politkovskaya, Stanislav Markelov and Natalia Estemirova. Finally, several independent media created in the 1990s, such as those owned by Vladimir Goussinski and Boris Berezovsky, have been punished, even to the point of having to give in to the authorities or close down, a trend that continues.

Invasion of Ukraine and war crimes

In February 2022, during the invasion of Ukraine, he was described by leaders such as Boris Johnson, Joe Biden and Jean-Yves Le Drian as a "dictator" and even a "butcher".

Conviction in court

On March 17, 2023, the International Criminal Court (ICC) (which has 123 member states and headquarters in The Hague, Netherlands) issued an international arrest warrant for Vladimir Putin and Maria Lvova-Belova for their involvement in and responsibility for war crimes committed in Ukraine since the Russian invasion. These war crimes concern the abduction, deportation, transfer and forced adoption of Ukrainian children. The arrest warrant was issued after more than a year of investigation by the Chamber. The ICC had initially decided that the warrants would not be made public. However, in order to protect victims and witnesses, as well as the investigation, it finally decided to publish them, as the crimes are still ongoing and "public awareness of the warrants can help prevent the commission of new crimes". The ICC points out that enforcement of the arrest warrants will depend on international cooperation .

Fortune

Various estimates (the highest ranging from $40 billion to $200 billion), have circulated over the years about Putin's fortune. For the *Washington Post* in 2015, "there isn't even a shred of evidence to support these estimates of Putin's fortune", and the paper notes that assets attributed to him (aircraft fleet, estates) may have been placed at his disposal. For the newspaper, the amount of these estimates is ultimately irrelevant, as Putin "has more power than money can buy".

Several allegations or accusations have been levelled at Vladimir Putin concerning an immense personal fortune amassed clandestinely through close acquaintances or former comrades; however, "there is little, if any, solid evidence to support these rumors and speculations" asserts *New York Times* journalist Peter Baker - which makes it impossible to accurately assess his fortune. The "*Panama Papers*" affair did, however, reveal that Putin's inner circle may have amassed several hundred million euros of public money.

Sergei Kolesnikov is a businessman who was asked by Putin, then deputy mayor of St. Petersburg, to co-direct a medical equipment company, *Petromed*. Kolesnikov claims that Putin, once in the Kremlin, offered Petromed major contracts on condition that he pay 35% of the proceeds to *Lirus,* a Luxembourg-based company. Some $500 million landed in Lirus' accounts, enabling Putin to build a 12,000 m^2 complex on the shores of the Black Sea, known as "Putin's Palace". Today, this residence officially belongs to one of Putin's close friends, businessman Alexandre Ponomarenko. Opposition politician Alexeï Navalny launched an investigation into this sumptuous residence in January 2021, claiming that the sale to Ponomarenko was fictitious and that the palace actually belonged to Putin. In particular, Navalny claims that President Putin has a "pathological" taste for luxury. Following the publication of the investigation, billionaire and businessman Arkadi Rotenberg, who is also close to Putin, claimed to be the current owner.

Russian political scientist Stanislav Belkovski claimed in 2007 that Putin was the richest man in Europe, with $40 billion in shares in gas (4.5% in Gazprom) and oil (50% in Gunvor) companies.

Boris Nemtsov, a former minister under Boris Yeltsin, claimed in a 2012 report that Putin owned palaces, villas, dozens of planes and helicopters worth a total of $1 billion, as well as yachts, hundreds of cars and a collection of watches. Putin's spokesman said that everything is state property and that Putin only has use of it. Boris Nemtsov added that $200 billion in gas company assets had been diverted to holding companies owned by Putin's front men, such as Yuri Kovalchuk, the brothers Arkadi and Boris Rotenberg and Gennady Timchenko.

In 2012, Vladimir Putin officially owned a 75-square-meter apartment, a studio in Moscow, two Volga cars and 135,000 euros. At the time, he declared an income of 100,000 euros. In March 2014, as part of financial sanctions against prominent Russians in retaliation for the 2014 referendum in Crimea that led to its attachment to Russia, a US government statement claimed that "Putin has investments in Gunvor and may have access to Gunvor funds".

In 2016, the *Panama Papers* directly named Sergei Roldugin, a close associate of President Vladimir Putin. In reaction to these revelations, Kremlin spokesman Dmitri Peskov considers that "this is about destabilizing the country. [...] I know there are other names - incriminated in the investigation - but it is clear that the main target of these attacks is our country and its president [...] There is nothing concrete or new about Putin, there are no details, and everything else is based on speculation".

On April 14, 2016, Vladimir Putin publicly admitted that the Panama Papers information about his relatives was true, but added that it contained nothing illegal. He accuses the United States of being behind the provocations and defends Roldugin, explaining that the latter "spent all the money he earned to buy musical instruments" and "got into debt with the funds through which he bought them". The following day, he made public his tax return according to which he earned 8.9 million rubles, or 118,200 euros, in 2015. He reportedly owns a 77-square-meter apartment, a garage, three Soviet-era cars and a caravan.

In a statement to the U.S. Senate Judiciary Committee on July 27, 2017, Bill Browder, co-founder of Hermitage Capital Management, claims that Vladimir Putin is at the head of a personal fortune of $200 billion, which he allegedly obtained by forcing Russian oligarchs to cede part of their assets to him. This sum, representing 10% of Russia's GDP, is said to be held in Switzerland, where it accounts for 10% of the total amount of foreign bank deposits.

In his nearly two-hour documentary, published on YouTube the day after his arrest, Alexei Navalny details what journalist Veronika Dorman describes as a veritable mafia system that enabled Vladimir Putin to become not only a multi-billionaire, but also the richest man in the world. This system also enabled him to enrich those close to him by taking money from the country's major industrial groups, many of which are in the hands of his friends.

Awards

Vladimir Putin is the recipient of numerous foreign orders and decorations:

- Order of King Abdul-Aziz (Saudi Arabia)

- Order of Friendship (China)

- Order of Zayed (United Arab Emirates)

- Gold medal of the Senate and Congress (Spain)

- Grand-croix de la Légion d'honneur (France)

- Grand Cross of the National Order of Merit (Guinea).

- Order of the Eagle (Kazakhstan)

- Order of the Liberator (Venezuela)

- Order of Ho Chi Minh (en) (en) (Việt Nam)

Other awards

- Honorary doctorate from several Russian and foreign universities, including India's Nehru University, Turkmen State University, the University of Athens and the University of Belgrade.

- *Time Magazine*'s 2007 Person of the Year (this title, which distinguishes the personality who has most influenced current events, for good or ill, is not considered honorary).

- Personality of the Year 2007 by Russian magazine *Expert*.

- Most powerful person in the world in 2013, 2014, 2015 and 2016, according to *Forbes* magazine.

- Winner of the Russian national "Peter the Great" prize.

- Winner of the 2011 Confucius Peace Prize.

- Honorary citizen of several Serbian towns, including Sombor, Požarevac and Apatin. Also decorated in March 2013 with the Order of the Republic of Serbia by its President Tomislav Nikolić.

Sports awards

- Judo, *rank*: black belt 8^e dan as of October 10, 2012 (awarded by the judo federation for his role as "perfect ambassador"); he is also honorary president of the International Judo Federation' . He was suspended in February 2022 following the invasion of Ukraine' .

Other books by United Library

https://campsite.bio/unitedlibrary

Printed in the USA
CPSIA information can be obtained
at www.ICGtesting.com
LVHW020549150524
780342LV00004B/557